RICKY HAS

A PROBLEM

Bill Vail

Illustrations by M.J.Reid

Chapter 1

Ricky has a problem. He thinks about it a lot. What he doesn't know is that it's a problem that a lot of other young people have too. It's the sort of problem that he cannot talk to any of his friends about.

It's the sort that he definitely hasn't been able to talk to any adult about, not even his parents or teachers, and not his big brother Sam. Ricky had thought about telling Sam, but he thought that he was too interested in other things to be bothered with him.

He thought about telling his best friend Jim, but he thought the better of that idea. Jim has a habit of blabbing out secrets to the wrong people!

How about hearing what this problem might be, I hear you say. Well, it isn't that easy to talk about, but here goes.

Maybe you didn't know this but when young people reach a certain age they begin to experience a thing called 'puberty'.

Pub-e what?

Yes, puberty is when your body goes through certain changes - physical changes and emotional changes. It is a natural part of maturing - becoming an adult. Everybody goes through this process.

For example, hair grows around your private parts and sometimes your privates can change according to the way that you feel. For a boy this is called an

erection. Like all boys Ricky liked
this feeling a lot.

Ricky was fourteen years old
and was going through his puberty.
He had worked out for himself what
had been going on with his body,
as a lot of boys do when no-one
else tells them.

Ricky watched a lot of
television and read a lot of
magazines. He stayed up late when
his parents were out and watched
some programmes that he
shouldn't be watching.

To tell you the truth he had
also been reading some of his
older brother's magazines that
were also not suitable for a boy of
his age. You know the kind, or
maybe not, but they have loads of
pictures of naked men and women
and they aren't playing football!

Sometimes when Ricky looked at these magazines, which was always in secret by the way, it made him feel quite good, very good in fact.

He really had to have a good look most nights. Before he went to sleep and first thing in the morning he would think about the pictures in the magazines. When he thought about these pictures he played with his own private parts, because touching his penis when he was aroused made him feel good.

The fact was that Ricky and his friends talked and joked about masturbating a lot and he knew that they all did it.

The strange thing was that when he was thinking about these images he often thought about other images that were not in the books or magazines. These thoughts, or fantasies as we'll call them, were of *young* girls and boys.

These fantasies are things that he really knew he should not think about but he did. Even if he tried not to think about them, he knew that sooner or later he would, as he enjoyed the feelings that he got from them.

Ricky was using these fantasies as his main thought for masturbating. When I say a main thought I mean that the images of the younger boys and girls were now a much more enjoyable fantasy than the pictures in the magazines.

The thing was that Ricky felt like masturbating more and more. He often wondered if anyone at

6

home noticed how much time he was spending in the bathroom.

Ricky wanted a girlfriend, he had heard his friends talk about the things they had got up to with their girlfriends and this made him jealous.

He didn't even know if their boasting was true, but in any case, he didn't have anything to boast about at all.

Ricky had never kissed a girl, in fact he wasn't any good around girls, well not girls of his own age anyway.

Chapter 2

One Friday afternoon he was on his way home from school with his friend Jim. It had been an ordinary kind of a day. Jim asked if he would come along with him to collect his younger sister Leanne who was at a friend's house.

This was the first time that Ricky had ever met Leanne. His first thoughts were that she looked much older than nine years old and that she was pretty. Leanne was a friendly sort of kid. Ricky thought that she liked him as she chatted away to him on the way home.

She wanted to hold Jim's hand but he told her to 'piss off'. At the same moment she grabbed Ricky's hand and for a few seconds he held on. Jim looked over at him and said:

'When are you two getting married?'

Leanne really laughed, but Ricky didn't think it was funny and told Jim to leave him alone.

Ricky thought about Leanne whilst he was masturbating that evening. He thought about her all Saturday morning and was actually wondering if she could be his girlfriend. Then he remembered that she was only nine years old and the stupidity of that idea hit him like a falling brick.

Jim rang and asked him if he would baby-sit with him that evening. Normally at a weekend he would sit up late surfing the late night channels on the television.

Tonight was another matter, as Leanne would of course be in Jim's house and Ricky found himself wondering about his next move. He wasn't even sure about his next move except that he knew that he wanted to kiss her and maybe more.

Ricky did not really look after his appearance but tonight he had put on his best shirt and cleaned himself up. Ricky called at Jim's house later that evening as his parents were leaving. Leanne was just going to bed as he arrived. Jim looked at Ricky and winked..did he know something? How could he?

'They'll be around in a minute, Ricky'.

'Who will?'

'The girls, you plonker,' Jim said.

Jim explained to Ricky that two girls from their class were calling at the house when the coast was clear.

Ricky had been quite relaxed up to that point, but he wasn't now.

If he had known this was a blind date he would not have had the confidence to be there. He wouldn't know what to say or do.

Charlene and Laura arrived shortly after Jim's parents had left. Jim appeared very cool and at ease in this situation, that was clear. It was not long before Jim and Laura were a mass of arms and legs on the settee.

Ricky felt very awkward. He was sure that the other girl did not fancy him, and to make matters worse he couldn't think of anything to say to her.

Ricky announced that he was going to the toilet.

'Going to make yourself beautiful,' said Jim.

Both he and his entangled girlfriend were highly amused by his obvious embarrassment.

Ricky went upstairs and found the loo, which was next door to Leanne's room. He knew that because there was a sign on the door which read LEANNE'S ROOM.

Chapter 3

Ricky wanted to go into the room, but he also wanted to go straight down the stairs and out the front door. He stood quietly looking at the bedroom door for what seemed like a few minutes.

Ricky went into the room and Leanne was still awake. She was looking at him. Her room was full of teddy bears and posters of boy-bands.

'What are you doing downstairs?'

'You shouldn't be in my room, you should have read the sign!' Leanne said in a slightly shaky voice.

Ricky left the room and went into the bathroom. He looked into the mirror and all he could see were his spots.

Ricky has a Problem
An Early Intervention Model with
Adolescent Sexual Abusers

Bill Vail

Professionals and parents are faced with a major challenge when confronted with adolescents who sexually abuse.

Parents often struggle to come to terms with their children's behaviour.

Professionals are faced with the task of engaging the young person in therapeutic work when most young people rarely discuss sexual matters with their parents never mind a worker who they don't know.

Ricky has a Problem is a work aimed at easing this transition for professionals and young people in a non-threatening way, whilst not avoiding the central themes of the work.

It also takes the first step to offering parents some insight into the behaviour of adolescents who abuse.

Bill Vail is a senior practitioner with Barnardos Young Peoples' Therapeutic Project based in Derry, N.I., having come to the project from a background of residential child care.

The following short story, *Ricky has a Problem,* is designed primarily to be an early intervention tool for the practitioner.

The young person should be encouraged to read the story, or to have it read to them, in sections. As a result, they may be able to identify with the subject of the story and, with help, recognise their own cycle of abusing behaviour. By hearing someone else's story, their own sense of isolation may be lessened as they may well have experienced similar events and feelings to the subject.

The practitioner may be able to use the story within sessions as a set of keys that will open discussion of a range of subjects with the young person. The design of the short story is aimed at early work within assessment where a non-threatening intervention is required, or when perhaps there has been difficulty in engaging the young person through other means.

The use of open questions is recommended to help the young person become involved in comparing aspects of the story to their own experience.

The messages within each chapter are intended to be as follows:

Chapter 1 This section looks at puberty and how it may affect a young person. It raises the subject of masturbation and also looks at sexual fantasy and inappropriate influences. It only highlights one form of unsafe fantasy as there needs to be careful discretion employed in making suggestions to young people in this situation.

Chapter 2 The relationship between grooming of the victim and the thought processes that accompany these thoughts and feelings are dealt with in this section. The idea of a cognitive distortion is introduced, i.e. that sex with a nine-year-old could be viewed as being acceptable. This section also looks at relationships with peers and the difficulties of overcoming shyness and low self-esteem. It explores how some young people cannot cope in certain social situations.

Chapter 3 The act of the abuse is carried out in this section. The chapter illustrates how the young person overcame both personal and victim resistance in carrying out the abusive act. It is clearly indicated to the reader that the young person had choices not to abuse and that the victim did not and could not give consent. The issues of power and manipulation of the abuser are highlighted. The use of physical force for compliance is also raised. Following the abuse the feelings of fear and guilt of the abuser are also illustrated.

Chapter 4 The completion of the cycle of abuse is followed through by the abuser by showing how the remorse and guilt have passed. It shows how the abuser again attempts to manipulate the thought processes of the victim causing her to doubt the loyalty of her brother.

Chapter 5 The disclosure of the event of abuse within the subject's family is illustrated in this section. The reactions of both sets of parents are shown as well as the legal consequences of the act. It outlines the negative realities of having been caught and the reaction of his family, friends and wider society. The benefits of treatment are shown in a way which would also indicate how difficult it can be to be in this position. The emphasis of treatment is shown to be the prevention of further hurt to other victims.

14

He knew that he wanted to go back into the bedroom and kiss Leanne. Nobody would ever know and he had convinced himself of this when he entered the room.

Ricky had the same feeling as he did when he read the magazines and had his fantasies. He moved quickly across the room and sat by Leanne on the bed.

'I told you to go away,' she said.

Ricky put his arm around her and said:

'It's OK, Jim asked me to check on you. Jim's lucky to have a sister like you. You're far nicer than the girls downstairs.'

Leanne looked as if she was about to cry, but Ricky didn't pay any attention to this and tried to kiss her. He put his hand under the quilt and tried to touch her privates.

Leanne told him to get out but he kept trying for a few minutes. Ricky knew that he was stronger than she was.

He had thought that Leanne wouldn't mind, but she just kept pushing him away. Ricky was really annoyed because he did not get what he wanted.

He got to his feet and left the room, but not before he had told her to keep her mouth shut about what had happened, as no-one would believe her anyway.

As he ran down the stairs a feeling of panic came over him, he could hear Leanne crying.

He was met by Jim at the bottom of the stairs who said:

'What's wrong with you, are you going to talk to this girl or not?'

Jim did not get a reply as he saw Ricky opening the front door in a hurry and leaving.

Chapter 4

Ricky was lying awake in bed the next morning. He was thinking about the previous night and had a good feeling when he thought about being in Leanne's bedroom.

He had made up his mind that he was going to call at Jim's that afternoon. Jim seemed glad to see Ricky and after he had explained to him that he had felt sick the previous night they began making their plans for the day.

Jim explained that he had promised his mum and dad to take Leanne to the park while they were shopping. It wasn't long before the three of them were on their way to the park. Leanne was staying close to her brother Jim.

Jim kept calling her a sticking plaster and pushing her in the direction of Ricky. Leanne wasn't enjoying this game but Jim could not see why she was in a bad mood.

When they reached the park they met some other lads from school. Jim went over to talk to them and quickly forgot about Leanne who was on the swings. Ricky sat on the next swing.

'I'm telling Jim about last night and you'll be in bother!'

'How will I be in bother? Jim knows I was in your room. He told me that I could do whatever I wanted to you. He thinks that you should grow up and be like the rest of the girls. Why do you think he kept pushing you towards me?'

Leanne looked really upset and before Ricky could say another word she jumped off the swing and ran straight for the park gate.

Jim walked over and asked what had happened. Ricky was worried that Jim would be angry with him but he was more concerned about his sister being on her own on the way home.

Ricky started to worry, he thought he had pushed things too far. He made an excuse to Jim and went back home.

Chapter 5

Ricky was right to be worried, as it wasn't too long before the sky fell in on him. Later the same evening it all started.

Ricky was in his room and there was a loud banging at the front door. When the door was answered he was in no doubt what was going on. Jim's father was shouting at his mum and dad. He was making it quite clear what had happened the previous night.

Ricky's parents did not say very much, they seemed to be in shock. Jim's father was so angry Ricky was afraid that he was going to come into the house and carry out the threats he was making at the front door. Jim's dad left shouting about, calling the police.

When Jim's dad had gone there was a lot of shouting and crying. His mum and dad were taking it in turns to do both. He had never seen his dad cry before. It was something he would not forget.

The fact that he did not deny the allegation, well not convincingly, seemed to upset them even more.

The police arrived at the house within the hour and they all had to go the police station. The neighbours all looked on with interest.

Ricky was terrified and ashamed. He tried to hold back the tears but that did not last too long. Ricky had never been in a police station before, but he was in one now and not enjoying the experience at all.

INTERVIEW ROOM

24

His parents warned him to tell the truth and not to mess about. He admitted everything to the police about having fantasies, watching those films and reading those magazines.

He did not believe he was actually saying these things but the officer seemed to have a way of getting the facts from him.

Ricky was charged with indecent assault and was told that he would have to go to court.

Ricky does not go out much these days. His friends do not call to ask him to go out any more. Everyone knows.

The last time Jim spoke to him in school he'd called him names and said that he'd ruined Leanne's life.

Ricky stays in his room a lot and thinks about the mess he's made of things.

He sees a special counsellor once a week since the incident happened and takes part in a group for boys who have done the same kind of thing. They talk about their problems and how things have worked out for them and for the boys and girls they have hurt.

The problem that Ricky had thought about so often he now has to talk about in great detail. It is not easy but he knows that it will help him not to behave in this way again.

Ricky actually feels a sense of relief now because there can be no more secrets.